TARAPUL, OH!

Tarapul, Oh!

A True Story Of A Sinner's Struggle

Craving forces Marriage Sins

By Paul Tarsleh

Paul Tarsleh
Tarapul, Oh!

Published by BooxAI
ISBN: 978-965-578-686-6

Contents

CAUTION

SPECIAL WORDS USED ACROSS MY BOOK

Heavens – The sphere in which God sits, plus all other spheres that make up the invisible world.

heavens – All other spheres, except the sphere (Throne) where God sits in the Spirit realm.

Heaven – The sphere for God, God's Throne, alone.

heaven – Any single sphere of the invisible world, excluding God's own.
Earth – Spiritual Earth that hosts the powers or forces that run the physical earth (hard ground).

earth – This physical ground on which we (solid humans) live.

** A sphere is the equivalent of one country in our human world. Each sphere has subdivisions.

Introduction

Every narrative in this book is a true story that took place in Liberia, West Africa, involving a teenager named *Tarapul*. The only thing that is shielded here is his real name and the real names of each character, including Lehana, who died of a severe ailment in 1992 during the Liberian civil war, and Beaticer, whose status, whether living or dead, has not been established since the war ended in 2003.

The teller of this story, Tarapul, lived unhappily throughout his life until he met me, the author of this book, in Planet Fitness (a commercial gym) on Watt Avenue in Sacramento, California, in 2017, with whom he shared this story from his heart.

We both started visiting each other until one evening when Tarapul met me writing one of my religious manuscripts. When he realized I was a writer, Tarapul obliged me to listen to his story, which he had long wanted to tell such a person. When he and I discovered that we had shared similar experiences, though in slightly different ways, and when we both saw what is happening to men in this world, we knew Tarapul's story needed to be told.

I have spiced up Tarapul's story with idioms like *"the journey of a night walk in the jungle of marriage"* to make other points that describe the mysteries Tarapul has encountered over the years.

I have also used Tarapul's story to illustrate the third sin category that God has given me and to explain "Business Marriage" as opposed to "Real Marriage" in the modern world.

God told me that whenever man calculates anything inside his heart before taking an action that the Bible frowns on, that act is called "conscious or intentional sin." Whenever man experiences a heart jump in the form of lust, for example, it's called "unconscious or unintentional sin." Whenever a man is forced, pressured, or commandeered by someone more powerful than him or her to do something wrong, the act becomes a third category of sin called "imposed sin," which is not labeled as such in the Bible. However, we certainly see examples of it there, such as Judas' betrayal of Jesus (Satan compelled him).

In this book, Tarapul has two marriages, but the one he has with Kutar is what he describes as a "Business Marriage" that he sees in this modern world as opposed to what he calls a "Real Marriage" handed down by God. He said a Business Marriage is entirely driven by business interest and has a concept of spending money on a partner to seek repayment from the partner, while a Real Marriage is a concept that is (should be) based on love that takes delights in spending money on a partner to uplift (complement) his/her wellbeing and in return, he/she spends money on the other based on the same mindset. He said when a business concept is employed in any marriage, marriage only survives when there is always money.

As the world draws near and near each day to the end, God has come back to review the word and to tell how judgment shall be carried on in Heaven after the end of all that mankind continues to do each day.

This book is one of several modern theocracies that tell us what God has for mankind at last. That's why imposed actions by Satan shall be his judgment in Heaven while man's acceptance of these impulses shall be his part of judgment.

In this book, you, the reader, shall see superscripted numbers that are attached to all the women Tarapul came across. These numbers simply count the women he has had his bad experiences with.

One important thing I don't want to forget is that this book is divided into two major parts – Physical and Spiritual.

The first part dealing with the life story of Tarapul is the physical one, while the Spiritual part deals with types of rape and their impacts on societies.

Tarapul's story is used here to prepare us physically for what we know is taken place on earth already, but to bring our focus to what is not most talked about when people talk about rape. When people talk about rape in most societies, they refer to men's ill- treatment of women, but they don't pay much attention to women's actions concerning rape. This low attention towards women's rape of men is most common outside the Western world.

Even in the Western world, men are often shamed and prosecuted more than the legal system does to women, but the legal system is low towards women's rape crimes because men have been silent on reporting their own cases. This is what happened in the US when one former US President was shamed, humiliated, and impeached for a sex crime, which eluded the fact that he was the victim of the act committed by the young woman who should have been guilty of raping the President had there been known what Spiritual rape is.

That President failed to speak out about what that woman did to him. Instead, the woman spoke out to blame the President for taking advantage of her. The media lashed out at that President as the perpetrator while hailing that woman as the victim. This book is here to reveal the truth.

So, the reason why the woman was not seen as the perpetrator is due to ignorance of Spiritual rape. The world doesn't know anything about Spiritual rape yet focuses on physical rape alone.

Physical rape is the act of one person performing sexual acts on another without their consent or full consent. However, there is another aspect of violation known as spiritual rape. This involves triggering, provoking, or invoking heavenly forces that exert power over humans. It occurs when a single human being initiates any sexual or sexually related acts.

Unfortunately, what humans often deem as crucial is sometimes of lesser importance to God because some issues are contingent upon others. That is why in these last days, Spiritual rape has become a significant concern for God due to the extensive damage it has inflicted upon the Church. This means that Spiritual rape, often perpetrated by women, has led to the downfall of numerous clergymen across churches worldwide. Therefore, it's now crucial to shed light on the concept of Spiritual rape. We will start by discussing the physical actions that women inflicted upon Tarapul, before delving into the trauma he endured.

Trauma is the constant flashes of the mind that continuously create an image in front of a victim of what had happened. So, Spirituality emerges to tell us what keeps bringing those images to the victim, not only a victim, but anyone who receives images that are often called reminders.

CHAPTER 1

THE TWO INNOCENT LOVERS

He walked a 45-minute road from the village to the town, Targbonma, to see her so they could play as usual. "Hoooooo! Hoooooo! Haaaaaaa! Haaaaaaa!" There is wailing and gnashing all over the place. He asked, "What's happening?" He rushed inside, but the crowd of old people, mostly women and a few elderly men, filled the sitting room.

"Tara, Tara, I want to see Tara." Janet grunted slowly while her mom and everybody continued to ask who Tara was. (Tara is the short way she calls Tarapul).

"Jan, Jan, Jan, Jan oooooh, Jan ooooooh." Her mom wailed louder and louder, rolling all over the floor and all the women dabbled here and there to hold her down. Some of them kept on fitting lapper on her while the older men took Janet's corpse to fix it up.

"Tarapul, Tarapul, Jan has been calling you!" One of her siblings, who knew Tarapul's relationship with her, rushed outside to tell Tarapul, who was peeking through the narrow window that every young person squeezed eyes through to see what was happening in there.

A beautiful 15-year-old Janet is dead. Nobody knew the cause of death since this was a primitive town where no medical facility existed to carry on postmortem. All fingers pointed to her uncle, who was known for witchcraft activities.

Tarapul, a 14-year-old boy, was devastated by his best friend's death. A strong love bond existed between the two until her demise. Even though the two were innocent of what intimacy was like, they felt it, yet they didn't make up until this tragic incident.

After Janet's burial, Tarapul found himself always troubled by Janet. Janet appeared in Tarapul's dreams every night, engaging him in playful activities. He laughed and giggled in his sleep as she tickled him, and they played hide and seek. In the morning, around 4 A.M., she came to wake him up to get ready for school, and when he tended to be tired, she pinched his sides and knocked his head so much so that he screamed and shouted, "Leave me, stop. I say stop! I'll hit you, too, though. Leave me, I'm tired!" Confused by his exclamations, his grandmother would ask, "Tarapul, who are you talking to? Tell me, what's going on with you?" But he wouldn't tell his grandmom the truth.

After a long while, Janet told Tarapul that they should go to her place. He wouldn't accept to go with her, they started to quarrel, and Janet started to use force on him, so he shouted, "Leave me. I don't want to go. I can't go with you. I'll tell my grandmom if you don't stop." Plaaap, plaaap, grand mom slapped him, "Get up!! Tarapul, Tarapul, it's been long since I've been asking you what is wrong with you, but you wouldn't speak out." His grandmom murmured to him. "Obviously, there is evil hovering around you, but we won't find a solution unless you open up to me." Said his grandmom.

Perspiration rolled down his face while breathing like a dog that just finished a race.

He said, "Mom, it's Janet."

"Who is Janet?" grandmom asked.

"It'ssss .... It'sss... it's Janet, the girl that died the last time."

"Holy Mary!" Grandmom shrugged and shouted (Grandmom is an Assembly of God (AG) church member). "So, this is what you've been hiding all this while?"

"Don't you know that she wants to carry you to the land of the dead, my son?" grand mom retorted. "It's okay, your father (Tarapul's grandfather) and I will see to it." She finished up.

Tarapul's grandmom and grandpa are both Christians, but they would use traditional herbs to drive out a dead person's manifesting spirit away from him.

In this culture, hunting spirits of dead ones are believed to be real, so there are traditional herbs that provide quick solutions to such problems.

Tarapul's grandparents didn't go for church prayers as should have been the case since they were Christ believers.

That day, Tarapul had to stay home from school to allow them to do the necessary things to let Janet's spirit go off him.

CHAPTER 2

TEENAGE ADMIRER

Tarapul has seen Alicia and he liked her so much in the town, but he lacked the courage to befriend her. Maybe one of the reasons was that she has older brothers than him and, you know, they often watched over her like night-watch dogs so that no boy fooled around her. That is because she was the Mamie Watta (having the beauty of a water lady) type who every man would want to devour. The second reason was that she was the mummy girl who was also too shy to mingle. Because of her, Tarapul didn't turn down any daddy's request that made him drop off something at Alicia's father's village.

Tarapul was yet 14, but inside him was an urge to do well what he experienced two years ago.

Two years ago, Tarapul was raped by his cousin, 25 years old, and that picture didn't leave his mind every time he saw a young girl. It was responsible for his closeness to Janet, while Janet was the one expressing fear about it even while she loved him. She postponed and postponed until she died.

CHAPTER 3

HIS COUSIN STARTED IT

Marybel was a student in Yekepa, Nimba County, Liberia. Her mom married her uncle after her father died. They lived in the same village where Tarapul lived with his grandparents. Every school break, she came to help her mom with farm work. Tarapul was one of the little ones she always commanded to do her chores. He called her big sister; the word 'cousin' didn't exist in this society.

She had been here for two weeks now. That night, she called Tarapul to come and sleep beside her so that she could have someone to awaken her whenever she had a nightmare. Poor Tarapul, what did he know to object, in fact, she was an elder sister to whom he couldn't say no. This was a village without electricity. The people here used lanterns that used kerosene. At night, some villagers quenched theirs while some had them lowered. That night, Marybel quenched hers to save kerosene and she asked Tarapul to get on top of her because she felt too cold. When he touched her, he felt her bare body, absolutely no pants and no bras. She took the blanket to cover two of them, but Tarapul still had no idea what was happening.

Then, she asked him to take off his pants as well, because it was hard-short jeans that hurt her body and, up to now, he remained obedient. However, something struck him when she started to touch him and finally held to his strong rod while instructing him on what to do. As you can imagine, he had no idea because there was no internet to watch videos, so she held onto his back and helped him reverberate. It was totally self-service to herself. He had no water in him yet. The next day, she left for Yekepa; maybe it wasn't worth it, or worse still, she felt ashamed.

Tarapul kept it as a secret because that's what he was told, but he felt sick inside due to his questions about what had happened and what he had done, so he wanted to venture more. From this moment, Tarapul doesn't know what age difference is about making love.

CHAPTER 4

HIS TRAUMA PUSHED HIM

So, two years after, when [1]Tybet, 19 years old, called Tarapul to come and sleep beside her while her 60-year-old fiancé was out of town, he had a little thinking about what was looming. Even though he didn't like Tybet, he wanted to know more about what happened two years ago. In fact, at 14, Tarapul could now see his own water, that man's fluid.

Tarapul didn't like Tybet, because everyone in the town called her "Cola" or "Village hallot," who served every visitor, but he thought she was more experienced to teach him more of what he didn't understand that night since Marybel didn't repeat it with him.

Tybet had been engaged to an old man since the first day her mom gave birth to her, so she was under parental obligation to marry him. She objected to him, but the pressure was on her. He had gone to another town to visit friends but didn't return for a week. It was just a few weeks before her marriage ceremony, so she was heavily monitored. She was not allowed to visit any girlfriends, but the friends were allowed to see her in the daytime. This was a precautionary measure to prevent her from running away to escape the marriage to her old man.

So, that night, she called Tarapul, whose parents lived next door to her parents. She planned with him on the day that she wanted him to come and sleep beside her because she was scared to sleep alone since her fiancé had gone out of town. That's why, at nightfall, she smuggled him into the house before her mom even left her peers' night gathering. Before bedtime, Tybet's mom came to inspect her room, and then she went to lock all the doors, but Tybet hid Tarapul behind the bed.

When they got in bed, Tybet said she wanted to turn off the lantern because she liked to sleep with no clothes on due to a heating problem in the house. She said the house remained hot until midnight or past midnight when cold had begun to come in, so if she kept her clothes on, she wouldn't have found sleep until late at night. Then she asked Tarapul if he wouldn't like to do the same. He agreed to do the same, knowing deep down his heart what was hovering around. To him, it seemed that this was what women did to men all the time. It seemed like a game that women played, but little children didn't know and now he wanted to take adventure. So, he removed his clothes just as she did, and they went to bed. As soon as they got in bed, she asked him to cuddle her because she was scared, so he followed her instructions. In his heart, he asked himself: *Did she forget that cuddling me would have given her more heat?* Then he laughed over the trick that he had already suspected.

Tarapul was now a grown-up boy whose rod stood up in his pants so quickly. So, it happened to him immediately, he cuddled her and then she cracked a joke at him, "Um, I didn't know that you were such a big boy, but it's good." There was the sound of feet coming closer, so she whispered to him,

"Keep quiet. Maybe that's my mom; that's what she does all night, thinking that I may bring a man in here."

"Tybet, Tybet? Uh, she's sleeping now, but I thought I heard a little noise in there.

Well, let me not disturb her. She had worked so hard today." Tybet's mom soliloquized.

"Uh... she's gone. Thank God." Tybet whispered again. "Tarapul, I know you're not a child now, so you can't say that you're scared of me. Come here, let's do something." She pulled him on top and granted him the access code.

This time, he knew what he needed to do, so he took his place as a man and after a long while, he completed his first ever do-it-yourself. Two or three minutes after break, he was up one more time, and she felt his strength, so she granted him access again.

That night, Tarapul received full knowledge of why and what his cousin needed from him. Tybet told him that she called him because she had been deprived of going out to see her boyfriend for over a week now. She told him that she didn't allow the old man to touch her, and she wouldn't ever allow him to do so, even if she was forced into the marriage. After this night, Tybet planned to arrange another smuggle in a few days.

Fortunately for Tybet, the old man didn't return alive. He died in the other town three days after he left his hometown and, before he gave up to the ghost, those who were with him said that he knew that he was about to go to the next world, but he only wanted to fulfill his dream of marrying the girl he had suffered for all the years, working for her parents every farming year and giving gifts all through those years she was a little girl.

As soon as the news reached their town, Tybet left for the

big city (Monrovia, Liberia) to escape the possibility that someone in the old man's family would continue troubling her in the name of tradition. Unfortunately for her and Tarapul, they didn't have a second time together.

Two years later, Tarapul left for the big city too. He didn't see Tybet in the big city because she had left for another area far away from the big city.

CHAPTER 5

TARAPUL IN LOVE WITH EVEREE

Janet and Tybet were Tarapul's quest for the knowledge of woman, but now Everee, it's a real thing what he felt for that woman. She's very slim and walks straight with shining black skin that Tarapul called her black chivy, a slang that he used to describe how attractive or enticing her black skin type was.

He was an eighth (8th) grader, and she was a sixth (6th) grader. He loved her so much that every recess, he ran straight down the stairs to ensure he didn't miss her before she went with her friends for recess. But Everee was very pompous or, let's say, arrogant towards boys, including Tarapul. He didn't like arrogance, so it upset him all the time she exhibited one, and even whenever she made him ashamed in front of her friends, he never stopped loving her, he never stopped waiting at her classroom door, he never stopped giving the recess money that she rejected at most times. His friends, Eratusu, Benobed, Dolomarkoma, and Davies, thought that he was too crazy about this one girl while there were other girls all around.

Every day, as soon as the school bell rang, Tarapul hurried

down the stairs to go out to wait for her at the iron gate so that he could walk her halfway to her home way before he turned around to go home. But there was just one thing Everee continued to say to him: she didn't want to accept him or any guy.

"Why?" He asked.

"Because I don't want any man, not because I don't like you." She replied.

Tarapul believed her when she said she didn't want any guy at all because he alone didn't receive insults from her. In fact, other guys just hated her. They thought she was too much for herself, too arrogant, cocky. They disgusted her a lot, but Tarapul wouldn't mind telling her how much he loved her.

After six months of chasing her and enduring her insults, she opened up to him, saying how she had been afraid to have an early pregnancy. She said, "I'm so afraid of men because I was raped before and I got pregnant. When I went to abort it, because I was afraid of my parents, I nearly died. That's the reason why I was sent from Ghana to my aunty in Liberia." It was shocking to Tarapul, and he pitied her. He agreed with her on having a fear of men's touch, but he promised to love her and make sure that she didn't get pregnant. She told him she was going to think about it, but it was not a promise. Little flexibility came between them, and everyone thought he had won her love.

Onc month passed and she couldn't accept to visit his place. Two months passed and she kept saying she was still thinking. Now, he thought she was making a fool of him. He got upset day by day and now his heart began to think of doing something extraordinary to her. Evil was now playing on his heart because everybody thought she was his girl, but she was not as far as he knew. He reduced the times he went to her classroom during recess and all her friends and his friends thought it was because he had caught her. They made jokes about two of them, particularly him, that he fought a fight to subdue her because she no longer insulted him and neither refused to walk with him on campus nor after school.

The third month has come to make it nine months since he had started chasing behind her. As soon as the school bell rang, she entered his classroom and walked straight to his desk. Everybody was looking at her, whispering to each other: *What is she doing here today?* That's the big question he asked himself, too. She collected his books and told him to come so that they could go home. He asked himself: *Which home is she going to?*

When they walked past the school gate, she told him she was going to his house if it was okay by him. She now handed him his book bag and they kept walking until they got to the intersection of the two streets where he usually left his direction to walk her halfway before coming back to go home. Approaching the intersection, he wanted to know which street she was going to take, but this time, she took the one leading to his house. Then she teased him, "You must be surprised, right?"

"Let's go, let me see your place," she said. He sighed, *um,* and they continued with their school lectures about their teachers.

When they got to his house, they went straight into his room (this belonged to his uncle, who had gone to work, but slept in the room with him all the time). She took off her shoes and went straight to the bed to relax while he grabbed from the fridge a bottle of soda (soft drink) for her to drink. He also took off his shoes and joined her on the bed. He bent on the side to grab her for a play, but she shrugged. He went for a kiss, but she shrugged again. "Can't we lecture quietly since this is my first time?" She asked.

He was on fire and couldn't listen. He continued to make attempts to set her on fire, too, but she didn't let him. And finally, she got out of bed to wear her shoes, but he wouldn't let her do so. He was all over her, rubbing himself all over her, telling her to let them get it done. She got tired of explaining herself and got angry at last, pouncing on the door and leaping out of the room. He jumped out to go after her to make her come back, but she continued her way. This was the end, but he didn't know until the next day.

Chapter 6

Everee crucified Tarapul

Early that morning, she handed him a letter. It was his crucifixion. In the letter, she wrote: "It's over between us. I can't bear to have you even an inch close to me again. You were too hot to control yourself and it's going to pose a danger to me if I let you have me. I came to your house only to test you, to see how much control you could exert over your feelings whenever you saw me or any beautiful girl. You were one of those men who can't control themselves to pass over a single night, even when their girlfriends or wives tell them that they're in their dangerous period or they're tired. I know very well that you love me, but you're going to pose a danger to my education. So, I'm asking you to kill the love you have for me."

Tarapul was devastated but held himself responsible for this because she had told him her reason for not letting boys in her life. All she needed was an understanding and self-control man.

CHAPTER 7

THE PASTOR'S WIFE DID IT TOO

Schools have closed and it is vacation time, so Tarapul returned home from the big city. He met [2]Nancia, who has also come from the big city. Nancia was the elder sister to Tybet, but she was the one Tarapul loved even before she left for the city. She loved him, too, but she had no idea what transpired between her little sister and Tarapul. Tarapul wouldn't tell her because he believed he didn't love Tybet, and in fact, he didn't approach Tybet, but she lured him.

Nancia was a beautiful girl who was now married to a pastor in the city, but she had come to her hometown for the Season celebration. Her husband was not from her hometown.

When Tarapul heard Nancia tell him that she was married to a pastor in the big city, his hope faded out because he thought a pastor's wife could no longer cheat. Still, Nancia's continuous talk about whether Tarapul has a girlfriend now or whether he thought she was too old to be a friend has baffled him.

At this time, he's scared to tell Nancia that he had loved her long ago before she went to the city and still felt the same way.

He thought that he would be committing a sin to make love to a married woman and talk less of a pastor's wife. Tarapul suffered an unsettled spirit inside his body whenever Nancia came around, or she sent for him to come to visit her. So, one day, he asked her whether married people have boyfriends or girlfriends, especially a pastor or a pastor's wife, but she threw it off the discussion and said, "Don't you feel something for me, or do you find my husband here?"

So, she invited him to visit her tomorrow night when all the people would be busy singing and dancing in the town square.

The next day, Tarapul left his grandpa's village for the town to visit Nancia as she requested. He waited till 9:00 P.M. when he crept on to her mom's house. Still, he kept in mind that she was a married woman he shouldn't be seen with secretly. He feared what the implication would be if he was seen having an affair with a married woman or a pastor's wife at that. But her own words of encouragement made him think that it was something that even pastors' wives do, so he could do the same, too, if it was right for her.

She had been home for long waiting for him when everybody had left the vicinity.

The moonlight was on that night, so she sat outside, drinking stout and eating bush meat.

She rushed to him as soon as she spotted him and involuntarily kissed him before he realized that it happened. Whatever fear he held had to go away now and he must face the demand of the urges that burned his body when two unrelated opposite sexes lurked themselves under a secret tree.

Without delay, they rushed into the house and, in a short moment, there was this sound of a scuffle, grunting, and moaning that filled the air inside the house. Once again,

Tarapul sensed the kind of passion or craving that Tybet and Marybel showed when they lured him into satisfying their bodies' desires.

He began to wonder why women were like this. Now was a question that shall bear hold of him forever because of what this married woman, in fact, a pastor's wife, had done. It began to take away his sense of respect and trust for what marriage should be.

They spent three months in the town and then they returned to their various communities in the big city, where they kept on visiting each other to continue their secret act.

Tarapul was initiated into the dubiety of women; the secret acts carried out on him by older women, so he came to get fond of having older women and married women.

CHAPTER 8

TARAPUL AS TEST EXAMPLE

So, he met [3]Beaticer, another married woman. This time, he had no more fear of how abominable it was to go unto others' wives. In fact, he thought they enjoyed it. He thought it was a game for them. He discovered the real reasons behind this act as he found Beaticer.

At 19 years old, Beaticer's mom gave her up to Mr. Silwon, who was 68. Mr. Silwon was a teacher at a vocational school in a municipal city who rendered help to Beaticer's mom in the little community where he lived, and when he saw the little girl, he started to buy things for her. Now, he wanted to keep her, but she refused and her mom thought her marriage to Silwon would be the best way to pay him back for all the good he had rendered to them. Beaticer didn't like the idea of an old man, but she had to obey her mom. Soon, Beaticer got pregnant for Mr. Silwon and she had to move in with him. There was no dowry or wedding, but Silwon called her his wife.

Oh Gosh, see how beautiful she is: she's black and plum with an enticing smile of white teeth in her mouth.

Silwon believed her beauty was too capitulating, so he

didn't allow her to give a smile to or talk to different men, no, not at all. He beat and bruised her for any attempt to speak with other men, particularly boys of her own age, so she kept indoors all through the day unless she got to go to the market or to see her mom, but in the company of Silwon's 10-year-old son, who stayed home with her while he's at work.

His son, Recinp, went to school in the afternoon when Silwon had returned from work, and once he was home, he never left the house till the next day when he had gone to work again. Because of Beaticer, he kept no friends; neither did he invite friends nor any other man into his exclusive compound.

There was Lehana, her husband, and kids living across the car road. Tarapul's stepfather's house stayed behind a thick bush that separated Silwon's house from his house, so Tarapul was like any other man or boy who saw Beaticer all the time, either on the street or while passing by Silwon's house. Beaticer only waved or spoke loudly to anyone that she wanted to greet while passing by, because she couldn't stop to have a conversation.

However, Lehana and Beaticer are from the same tribal village, so Beaticer is seldom allowed to visit Lehana, but only when Silwon is home, sitting outside his house to overlook them in Lehana's compound. While the two sat there to keep company and any man visitor came by to Lehana's, Beaticer was bound to leave until that visitor would have left before she returned if she so desired to continue with her company with Lehana.

But on one lucky day, Tarapul got Mr. Silwon to accept him into his compound. On this godly afternoon, Silwon was struggling to dig dirt to fix bricks to remodel his little old house and Tarapul came passing by. He saw Silwon turn his back towards the alley, so he left the alley that headed up to his friend's parents' house and branched out to Mr. Silwon. Then grabbed the digger quickly and, with all the young energy, began to punch into the ground before Silwon ever looked. When Silwon saw him punching into the ground, he said nothing, unlike usual. Tarapul spoke no word, but kept on digging and digging and digging; then, he grabbed the shovel to pile up the mud and went on to the brick machine to start molding the bricks. Mr. Silicon grabbed his chair and did nothing, but watch Tarapul do the work he had readied himself to do with his old joints aching.

When Tarapul looked over his shoulder towards the kitchen, Beaticer was standing and chuckling. Little Recinp, too, spoke no word, but continued staring and smiling. Then Silwon called to Beaticer, and when she came, he told her to grab a big rooster from his small poultry to kill it. When she asked, he told her to go ahead since she had no eyes to see the hard-working young boy.

Tarapul pretended not to know what was going on. He just continued to work harder, but inside his stomach was a lump of joy that told him that Silwon had been overcome.

Then Silwon broke the silence, "My son, you may come and rest. I have water here and I have liquor here too. Choose whichever you want." He called to Tarapul, but Tarapul pretended he wasn't tired yet, so he said, "Sir, I'll be there in a little moment."

About 30 minutes after Tarapul was called, he just went to take a little rest. "Mr. Silwon, you could have called someone like me to help with this kind of work. It's not good for you and it's tedious for your age and status. I mean, we're all neighbors and we should help each other." Tarapul sympathized with old man Silwon.

"Oh, thank you, my son, for being so good to me today. I

didn't think I could have done this work today as much as you're doing right now. I appreciate it." Silwon replied.

Tarapul sat and drank a cup of icy cool water and he took a bottle of small beer. He kept on peeking at Beaticer without letting Silwon see him, but said nothing to her. He made no attempt to notice her, even when she brought a little ice block to put into the water that was in a pitcher to make it cold for drinking. Only a little Recinp boy could talk with Tarapul like his father did.

All this while Tarapul deliberately acted as if he had never spoken with Beaticer before, but indeed, he coincidentally met her several times at Lehana's house whenever he went there to eat.

Tarapul has been helping Lehana's husband, Manfre, to maintain his yard every time the grass overgrew, so Lehana has been giving food to him and this indirectly turned Lehana's house into the second home for Tarapul.

From the start, each time Tarapul met Beaticer in Lehana's house, she got up quickly to leave the place, but one day, Tarapul managed to tell her his feelings when he met her there while little Recinp was somewhere around playing with Lehana's kids. She accepted him and they became lovers.

So, the truth was, before this renovating day, they were lovers already, which means they both really had some secrets hidden from Silwon before he offered his big rooster.

Tarapul returned to work, and after a very long while, like four hours, Beaticer told her husband that the food was ready. He told her to set the table. Then, he called Tarapul to come and take something solid for the stomach since he'd been working this long.

Tarapul hurried to the little table that Beaticer brought out near the workplace and he sat to eat.

The big bowl is filled with chicken, so Tarapul is shocked. Silwon notices him, so he tells him that everything is for him alone. Tarapul was free to eat it all or take any remaining food to his house. So, Tarapul ate and then told little Recinp to prepare the remaining food that he would take along after work. "No, no." Recinp was very careless. "Just leave it and B (this is what he called his wife) will come and do that." Silwon interrupted.

Tarapul returned to work after some 15 minutes of rest, and in the next one hour, the work was done entirely with the accompanying hands of Mr. Silwon, who handled the minor parts of the entire process, like pouring water whenever Tarapul needed it and greasing the Mold whenever brick got stuck in it.

All this while Beaticer was cooking, she never stopped laughing at her husband whenever she looked at Tarapul from the kitchen. They two enjoyed themselves, making a mockery of her husband throughout the time he stayed working for Mr. Silwon.

At last, he took his food and told Silwon a farewell without uttering a single word to Beaticer. All thank you for the food went to Mr. Silwon. This was how they made fun of him for obvious reasons.

This pretense of help was to gain access to visiting Beaticer any time, even if Mr. Silwon was at home or not. It created a flexible means where Recinp wouldn't serve as an obstacle anymore to Tarapul going into the yard whenever he wanted to, and from that day, he had always visited Mr. Silwon by sitting to hold little lectures with him without showing a sign of any notice of Beaticer, even whenever she passed by in her usual way of doing house chores.

It was all tricks to seeing each other faces even whenever they didn't want to have fun.

It was on Saturday, so they did not see each other until Monday afternoon when Tarapul had come from school to go to Lehana's house to eat in his usual style. Lehana's house or her food has become so used to him for the past six months now because his stepmom was not good to him. She took her anger at him for every little thing, because she didn't approve of his mother being a mate, so she nagged all the time and refused to serve him food right.

It was Lehana who worked between Beaticer and Tarapul, offering her room for their meeting almost every afternoon, when Silwon fell asleep in the hammock that hung right outside to make him look directly across the street to Lehana's yard. At least Beaticer had studied her husband for an afternoon nap all through the two years she stayed with him. No matter what, he fell asleep around 4:00 P.M. and stayed asleep until 5:00 P.M. every day. This was a body routine that he was taught when he was a young child living with some rich couple in the big city back in the 60s and now, she found a boyfriend, so she was set to exploit his sleeping time.

So, Beaticer quickly came to Lehana's house to meet Tarapul that Monday afternoon as soon as Silwon fell asleep and she congratulated Tarapul for the fool he'd made of her husband yesterday. They burst into laughter and Beaticer revealed her purpose of cheating on her husband. She said she had later accepted the fact that she was now forced into an inappropriate marriage, but she later discovered that Silwon loved, cherished, and pampered her very much. When she looked at most young couples, she found out that they didn't have the amount of peace that she enjoyed with an old man. Therefore, she resolved to love him back, but he had become overbearing with his jealousy; jealousy that made him always accuse her falsely, beat her every time for the wrong reasons and, the worst part, deprived her of seeing all her young girlfriends that she had before meeting him. As she put it in her words, "I choose to test the water to know if he actually had all it takes to stop me from having a boyfriend if I wanted to, so I looked among you, the young boys in this community and I came to love you, even before you ever told me that you love me. Now I found out that he was a big fool and that I also have all the time he stays at work to do anything that I could do IF I wanted to." She joked with all her teeth out.

Tarapul and Beaticer stayed in their game until Silwon got a government transfer back to the big city where he previously chose to stay as soon as he returned from a government scholarship study in India.

CHAPTER 9

LEHANA, THE HARDEST

Tarapul has already taken Lehana for a mother who fed him and a friend who made it possible for him to get the girl that he wanted. He took her husband, Mr. Manfre, for a father too and he thought he owed them an appreciation that he hoped to show by helping them with the little work that he could do for them. But this one, mmmm, urrrrr, it's another abomination like taking a pastor's wife.

Oh, women, women, what is wrong with them! When Beaticer left, [4]Lehana jumped behind Tarapul.

On a bright day afternoon, he was overpowered by Lehana, who came from the bathroom and entered her room to cream herself. Suddenly, she shouted in the room and called to Tarapul, "Tarapul, Tarapu, come, please come quickly!" He rushed into the room, only to see her locking the door behind him when he ran past her standing behind the door.

She's standing there naked like she was when she fell from her mom's womb. He was so shocked and terrified, and here again, he came to realize another luring attitude. Then he said to himself: *Is this their nature?*

Lehana flung herself at him, telling him to come and do what he used to do with Beaticer that she never stopped talking about it. There was an intense scuffle as he tried to resist her, but she grabbed his pants and threatened to levy a crime on him if he failed to comply.

Tarapul didn't go to school that day, but her three kids were still in school, so she had all the time to her advantage. Now Tarapul realized that if someone came around her house, he or she would hear their whispering noises and may leak it out to her husband. So, he remembered Joseph's story written in the Bible, but thought that he may not be lucky enough to liberate himself if it got out to her husband and the public. He gave in to let Lehana have her will.

After an hour, Lehana apologized to Tarapul, but admitted that she had been jealous of Beaticer for having him, because she kept telling her often that he satisfied her so much more than the old man did. She accused Beaticer of bluffing to her about Tarapul's strength when Beatricer knew that she didn't have such a person for herself, even while Manfre, her husband, was such a lazy man who only had her once or twice in a whole month.

Then she signaled to him for another round, saying, "This time without a fight, please!"

Well, the damage had been done and Tarapul knew that he was in it already, so what was there to fear other than to replace Beaticer with a hot friend who offered herself just like that?

He took a deep breath to upload enough energy for the new war just at hand and, in a few minutes, grabbed her, thrust her into her own room and let her feel what she craved to get.

She had a separate room opposite her husband's own. She said this was what her husband did to run away from her.

There was too much demand for him and she had been craving to have someone like him all this while.

She thought God had made it possible for her to get him by peacefully taking Beatricer out of the way, when he asked her about how she intended to put up with her own desire for him if Beaticer was still around.

She said, "I was just a few yards away from doing exactly what I just did without letting Beaticer know or being hurt."

From this day on, Lehana proved a diamond stone, a metal that couldn't be injured by any other, but remained that which always breaks others.

She made bush roads through the bushes surrounding her house and did the same thing through the bushes around her rice farm so that she could leave her husband at any time to meet Tarapul at the southern point whenever she entered into the bush, through the northern end.

The area here was a new community where few houses were built with distance well apart. There was no parboiled water line yet, but an electrical power line left the central city and passed through to go to a major government facility.

Her husband, Manfre, loved music very well, so every day when he came home from work and finished helping his kids with their lessons, he spent the rest of his time drinking cane juice (a local drink produced from distilling sugar cane water) and playing music in the sitting room to dance with his three kids or went out to see friends. And while he did all of this, she was either in the kitchen making some fresh meat or fresh fish pepper soup for everybody, or she went across the street to Beaticer when she was here, or she'd gone to visit someone nearby.

So, when she'd gotten Tarapul, it was easier now for her to enter the bush at any time to have him. They did this each time he came to their house to spend time with them. He often joined Manfre and the kids in their dances after they had all drunk the pepper soup and later pretended to be gone home after she had signaled her readiness. He did this by going eastward to his stepfather's house way, but later jumped into the bush to go around their house towards the West, and when they met in the bush, they often chose to stay on the West or go North or South to have fun.

There were pigs that ran through these bushes and they were very noisy, so Lehana and Tarapul used their noises to their own advantage. This meant that if someone was in the same vicinity and heard a sound of what seemed to be the voice of a human being, that person wouldn't have bothered at all, because it may have been that of a pig or a herd of pigs. That's why the two of them left a bush path and went crawling under a thick bush, like the pigs did, to go to a spot prepared under a broken bush, where they spent one or two hours having multiple rounds.

After the day rounds, Lehana may have still wanted another when night came, so the only way she got him to herself was the time she went at night to the kitchen that was built separately from the house. While she was there cooking, he often told Manfre and his kids good night, then went around the house to the kitchen, from where they two had a good time right behind the kitchen where she kept a flat iron sheet used for drying fish or rice.

One night, while they were here, the rain came pouring down and Tarapul wanted to jump out, but Lehana didn't let it happen. She had all her fingers pulling him down from his back and told him not even the rain had the power to end it.

At this moment, Tarapul realized that he was heading for doom. He thought to himself, a woman who couldn't let him go when there was rain pouring down on them could allow them to be caught. So, from that day, he decided to take control of the situation, choosing when and where they would meet, so she wouldn't have control over him anymore.

Probably, this prevented him from being caught until he left and, the last time he heard from her, was after a few years when the news of her death was released.

But during the period all this was going on, Lehana proved more terrible when she chose to accept Tarapul's stepfather, whom she said had been behind her for a very long time before she took Tarapul into her life.

It happened one evening when she told Tarapul that they could extort money from his stepfather if he could allow her to accept him since he didn't want to give up on her. Tarapul told her he wouldn't mind at all for as long as she had no problem with having the two of them in her life at the same time and for as long as she would allow him to have a greater share of whatever she got from him.

This is the deal, because Tarapul's stepfather was a big businessman, so he thought it was a good idea to use Lehana to get more money from him since he hardly gave enough money to Tarapul.

Lehana, too, didn't want to let Tarapul get out of her life because he was free to get to at any time, unlike his stepfather, who was married and conducted his business out of town for one or two months before coming to town. While at the same time, she realized that she needed his stepfather, who had been enticing her with huge sums of money.

She also knew that she had given Tarapul a large portion of her time, so it would have been difficult to have another man and hide that man.

Therefore, they sealed this deal and Tarapul went for

Ferninda, his stepfather, this night while Lehana's husband was out to see friends.

Ferninda was shocked when Tarapul told him that Lehana wanted to see him. He pretended that he had no secret with Lehana, but Tarapul told him that he knew everything, so he promised to keep everything secret for only three of them. Therefore, he urged him to go quickly, because her husband was not in yet, the kids were in bed and she was waiting. He accepted, so they went together to the house. When they got near the house, Tarapul told him to go in while he Tarapul would keep watch.

In a few moments, he came out and said thank you to Tarapul, and when Lehana came out, she called Tarapul to come and finish her as usual.

From this day on, Tarapul took control of the two people. He collected money from his stepfather any time and gave Lehana 40% of whatever he got. He told his stepfather how much Lehana said she wanted, then in return, told Lehana that he had requested X amount from her money boy. She agreed with everything he said and that's how he managed to dictate the time and place of their encounter without her showing off her careless attitude.

When Tarapul's stepfather came into Lehana's life, he learned about a good number of other men that he knew were passing by all the time, going to their different workplaces to be the ones she used to flirt around with.

All this he got to know when he accepted to share her with his stepfather. She felt comfortable telling him all her dirty deeds, saying that she used these men to fill in the gap of her husband, who was not up to the task.

Asked why she kept him as a husband, she said she loved him, but mostly due to his previous financial status that she used to take care of her needs and her family's needs, which has deteriorated recently. "All those guys coming around me are either married or cohabiting, so I used them just to satisfy myself. But now I have you, a free young guy. What else do I need them for when they're government workers who are as broke as my husband?" She concluded.

See the height of absurdity.

CHAPTER 10

SHE'S THE BRIGHT MOON, HE THOUGHT

Tarapul's grandfather's sick news got to him and he had to go to see him. Unfortunately, he passed. Tarapul stayed back to take care of other things before going back to the city, and there was Bonenoh, a bright, shining-skinned girl from the other town. She's keeping to a man, though.

When he saw her first, his heart leaped in him, because he thought she was the bright moon that he could have to brighten his time while he stayed in the interior. Soon, his friend told him that she was married. Tarapul gasped out that sound of regret and agreed to let a married woman go this time.

These married women have turned Tarapul into a playboy now, so he could recognize them as soon as he saw one that was eyeing him.

That's exactly what happened when Tarapul went to visit his friend Tinnahe, who lived in this town, and while they were keeping company, this bright girl came to greet his friend and also him, whom Tinnahe had spoken highly about.

She went away only to come back to ask Tinnahe, "Do you need something for your friend?"

Tinnahe told her, "Bring some bananas." She brought some and went back to her house.

After, like, 30 minutes, she came back to ask the city boy what the city looked like now since she left there two years ago. So, they chatted over the city's issues briefly and then she went back. After some time, she came back again, shouting at Tinnahe as to how it seemed he truly liked his friend. She thought they were staying too long, keeping him company, and Tinnahe must have forgotten that he had some things to do. He told her that he had decided not to go anywhere that day, but to use it to welcome his friend, whom he had left in town two months ago. Right after she left, Tarapul told Tinnahe to see him off and he left without telling her farewell.

When Tinnahe came to visit Tarapul two days later, he told Tarapul how Bonenoh got upset when she found out that he left that day without a farewell. Then Tinnahe sent his little brother into the room to bring out the dry fish Bonenoh had sent to him, Tarapul. He chuckled deep inside and said to himself; another trouble is hovering around me again.

When all the people came to town for the weekend, Bonenoh, who lived in the other nearby town, came to greet Tarapul directly to his own house. She brought another dry fish and told him how he needed to eat well before returning to the city. Now he made inquiries from her about her fiancé, and she told him, "I know Tinnahe didn't close his mouth and now he has told you all about me; so, what else I need to tell you, if not that my friendship doesn't matter to you more than what is behind me?", she murmured to him.

She said to Tarapul, "Yannaton was her lover, but not her husband, as people called it. So, you should stop asking about

Yannaton." Right there, this playboy confirmed his suspicion, so he told her that she was beautiful. Then, she thanked him and both parted their ways.

When the following week came, on Wednesday, she left her fiancé in the garden to come to the other town to visit Tarapul. When he saw her, he wasted no time but to serve her the purpose. She slept at his house that day and returned the next day.

While her fiancé (husband as they called him) and the other people continued to search for her on the farm, Tinnahe came straight to his friend's town, which was about an hour and a half walking distance, to find her, because he believed that she came to Tarapul, but didn't tell him. So, when both met on the way, she told him everything that happened then he passed her to come to Tarapul to warn him to be careful.

At this time, Tarapul paused to think about himself as to what was happening to him. He talked to himself, saying: *I'm not very handsome, neither do I have money, nor do I have a rich background somewhere that people know of. So, what is it about me that is appealing to women?*

Up to the time Tarapul gave his story to me in 2017, he hadn't found the answer to his past.

Bonenoh kept coming any moment she found them, but Tarapul told her to be very careful, because he did not intend to break into somebody's home. He told her that she only had herself to blame on any day that her fiancé got to know what she was doing outside their relationship, but she made jokes about it like, "Well, whenever he sees me, then he is free to make his own decision, aaaah." She laughed.

Her fiancé, Yannaton, had already gathered every bit of information about her and Tarapul, so on this day, she dropped his food off in the garden about 30 minutes away from their house and told him that she was not feeling well enough to stay with him. A few minutes later, his little sister came running to him and told him that his wife was getting dressed up to go to the other town. So, Yannaton left the food untouched and came running straight to the village (the people here called it a town). She had left before he got to the village, so he waited until nightfall when he went to the next town (now this is a real town), where he saw his wife in bed with Tarapul.

When Yannaton called his wife from the window to come out, she looked at him without panic and went for the window to close it to prevent him from entering. Nevertheless, he burst it open and entered through the narrow window.

Earlier, Tarapul had been sitting at the table inside his room when he suddenly saw a shadow that casts darkness from the moonlight. He talked briefly about it, but thought that one of his neighbors had passed by. It was when Yannaton pierced through the window, squeezing his short body to enter, that Tarapul realized the battle had reached him.

Yannaton went for his wife and they two began to fight. When Tarapul saw that it was really her fiancé, he took a firm grip of the knife in his hand and managed to open the room door. Then, he got out of the room to open the outdoors and, finally, ran out of his own house, leaving the two of them there to fight. One thing he noticed before leaving was that Yannaton didn't seem to have the capacity to overpower his fiancé to beat her like a man would.

Tarapul wished that Yannaton had the ability to beat Bonenoh very well to teach her the lesson that she needed to learn about cheating and disrespecting a husband or a half-husband. After all, he had warned her several times to stop the relationship, because he was not going to marry her, but she stubbornly refused and kept coming for more. Perhaps she couldn't get better than him.

A few months later, Bonenoh left her fiancé and went to an unknown destination.

Really, Bonenoh was not the only married woman that Tarapul was having fun with within the area. As you know by now, this was the way he was groomed by them, but she was the only one very disrespectful to her own. In this town and in the neighboring towns, there were other unimportant women who played safe with their marriages like Beaticer and Lehana did, and as the story continued, Bonenoh was yet to leave his life.

By this time, Tarapul had concluded that women weren't trustworthy and he also didn't think that marriage was worthy of trust. So, he continued to find meanings in marriage as opposed to the vows that are pronounced to each other during the ceremony time. He kept on thinking about the reason why people fool each other in the name of marriage vows that they know they can never keep. He was afraid to get married, because he thought it would all come back to him too, meaning he would always think of all the fake smiles his wife would put up for him after seeing someone.

CHAPTER 11

A TURNING MOMENT FOR TARAPUL

Tarapul came across Alicia at the same time Bonenoh suckled from his reservoir and he began the journey of a night walk in the jungle of marriage.

He went to visit this guy in the town and while they were keeping company in his room, this girl cracked open the door to bring food for the guy. Tarapul was startled at what he saw. "She is one of them." The guy whispered to Tarapul.

Tarapul quickened out and told him that he was going to be back later. The girl was one of the guy's numerous girls in the town.

What Tarapul saw in there was his long-lost childhood friend, Alicia, who used to be guarded by her numerous brothers way back before she traveled out of the town. She was the one he admired when Janet died, but he didn't talk to her at the time because he had no chance to do so, but he has been wishing to see her one day. Alicia doesn't recognize Tarapul in the first encounter in her boyfriend's room, but she shall do so later.

Three months after that day, Tarapul finally met Alicia and

introduced himself, only to see her shouting in the street. She told him where she went that time and under what condition she left. So, he wasted no time to let her know that he should have been her first love, but her people took her away and now they were back to their hometown. So, he said it was time to do the expected. She giggled and said nothing but told him bye.

Two days later, he paid her a visit and they talked lengthily. Then she told him that she had just suffered heartbreak and was struggling to recover, so she didn't think it was the right time to talk much about the issue.

He left and came back the next day... and in the next day... and the next day.

Now, he turned this into pressure on her, because he thought she might leave town soon without being able to see her again, so he needed to grab the chance, especially because she needed a comforter until then. Her boyfriend had broken her heart, so she was distressed.

One evening, he had managed to enter her room when her little brother told him that she was inside sleeping. Tarapul asked her little brother to direct him to her room and the boy did so, because he had seen Tarapul around lecturing with his big sister, so he thought that they were in a love relationship already.

Luckily for Tarapul, the room door was not locked, so he entered and before she opened her eyes, he was seated on her bed. She got up and asked, "How did you enter my room?"

He said, "God had made the day possible for us to spend time together. That's why your little brother let me in."

She didn't like it at all, but she refused to stand her ground to ask him out, that which he expected of her, but she kept calm and started receiving lectures from him.

Now that they were consumed in their solitary position, he

began to fondle her and there was this voice of "Stopppppp. Stopppp! I don't like it, though." And, not before long, there was the silence of normal speech-making, but a foreign language filled the air that pointed to the matter of mesmerizing.

On this day, Alicia took in and, in two months' time, her father would get involved and there would be trouble for Tarapul. Therefore, Tarapul had to perform the engagement rites and he had to take Alicia unto himself as his cohabitant. Once this was done, Alicia had become Tarapul's wife, so to speak.

Now, Tarapul has a wife (a cohabitant) who carried his first child. He had to love her and commit to her. She was very beautiful and bright like Bonenoh, but taller than Bonenoh's hair with long wasting hair.

Of all the women Tarapul had met, Alicia seemed well-reared and reserved, which set her apart from most women.

From all observations, she appeared to be committed to any man that she chose to be with and this was the kind of woman that Tarapul had long wished for. He was beginning to think that there were a few good apples amongst the numerous rotten apples he had ever seen.

In fact, her composure and continuous criticisms of her fellow women that she saw flocking around Tarapul and his friends, even when he didn't ask for them, assured him that she abhorred this promiscuous lifestyle. This made him think that she could make a perfect wife for him to keep him committed to marriage, but sooner would he know something that threatened his ability to keep her alone. It was her inability to keep up with his sexual demands.

Chapter 12

Bonenoh is back

After the birth of their first child, they had to travel to another city where Tarapul met Bonenoh again. She had a fiancé again, but as soon as she laid her eyes on Tarapul, everything between them went sour. This time around, she came begging Tarapul for marriage to be his second wife.

She went to Alicia to remind her that Bonenoh was there before her, so she would rather give in or accept to have a companion because, this time, she wouldn't let Tarapul go.

It was very challenging for Alicia and Tarapul, because Tarapul had just made the biggest mistake again by sleeping with Bonenoh. But, can you blame him? Alicia took a whole week or more, not letting him while accusing him of liking sex so much and, at one point, telling him to go find someone out there to help her!

However, it was not acceptable to Tarapul to keep two women as his wives, especially Bonenoh, whom he had already branded as a cheat and cunning, like Tybet, Nancia and

Lehana, who have all groomed him to be a cheat and a womanizer.

He thought she was good to be what she was, the one who ran after men even when they didn't seem to notice her. He thought if he kept her, she would do to him what she did with her two fiancés.

After all, Alicia thought if he had a girlfriend out there, it would have brought little freedom to let her have her long periods of sleep at night without him bothering her. So, he felt better about keeping Bonenoh for what she was good for.

Regretfully, Bonenoh had to give up her second wife's marriage request to find herself another guy.

And yet, after three years, Tarapul met Bonenoh again when he traveled out on a business trip where she hosted him in the house of her third or fourth or fifth fiancé, who knew nothing about their past except that they told him that they were from the same town.

When her fiancé left home each day, she came begging for Tarapul to make love to her, but he refused, saying she must respect her fiancé and put a total end to whatever she had for him, especially when her fiancé was hosting him for a goodwill gesture.

CHAPTER 13

ONE OF THE LOVE KILLERS

Alicia refused to go to school after stopping in third grade before meeting Tarapul, but chose the path of making children by eliminating the use of contraceptives all the time, and by this singular behavior, Tarapul was compelled to abandon the path of higher education in law that he had ever dreamed of after high school.

In every manner to take care of her and the kids, Tarapul found himself medium jobs here and there. Surely, his choice of staying with Alicia was based on sympathy and fear of causing her hardship during pregnancy or hardship in single motherhood.

She got pregnant seven different times, but now had three living children, forcing Tarapul to have more than he ever wanted.

Later, Tarapul tried to advance himself through the company's vocational study and got a mechanical engineering job at Bong Mines Iron Ore Company in Liberia.

While he worked, Alicia took care of their three kids, and as a typical African woman, she also took good care of her husband by doing all the cooking and serving whenever he returned home. Oh, she pampered him, showered him with love and it has been like this even when he didn't have a good job when they first met 15 years ago. With her, Tarapul enjoyed the kind of respect that was due him as a man of the home.

Unfortunately, Tarapul's love for Alicia faded slowly, as he was caught between imposed responsibilities for childbearing and his conscience of not letting her suffer alone.

Everything about her grew odd to him since she chose not to understand the problems connected to having more children in modern times.

CHAPTER 14

EVILS HAUNT OWNERS

Throughout these years and with all her assurances, Tarapul never stopped feeling that his wife would cheat on him. He thought that she was a pretender, just like the women who cheated on their husbands with him, even while they showed greater love to their husbands.

His heart was always pounding whenever she went to the market, especially when she took so long to come back home, where he often called her and her phone rang for so long without picking up. Oh no, he got close to having a heart attack. When she arrived home with her apologies or explanations for whatever transpired in the market or wherever she went, he got furious about all that, thinking that she was just making up stories about her whereabouts.

"Ha, ha, ha, ha! Ha, ha, ha, ha!" She burst up into laughter and teased him, "Jealous man, you think I'm like you, who doesn't get tired of sex and doesn't sit home with me, leaving your wife to fool around with other women? If I mind you, I will stay in the street with all those fools like you are looking for every woman that passes by, but you're blessed to have me."

She threw jokes at him, then she appeased him, saying, "My husband, I can't satisfy you alone, so what's the need of me going out there to get another new guy who wouldn't mind if he's hurting me or not? So, calm down, my dear." That's how she would leave him with a wrinkled face like a vicious lion in his state of worries and confusion. Then she would go to do whatever she had to do.

Tarapul lived in constant fear of young boys who came around his house, whether they were visiting friends of his children or whether his wife called for help from any one of them. He just didn't trust what they were capable of doing to his wife.

This fear included a constant watch over the movements of his own friends around his wife, sometimes making him place limitations on her closeness to any friend of his.

This fear also triggered his limited desire for having more friends and free participation in social life, like attending wild parties very often, inviting friends, or visiting them regularly and it remained his biggest secret that he had never told anyone since his experience with women in his teen and early twenties.

In fact, the same fear of women's cunning behaviors towards those who eat on the same tables with their husbands, stopped him from visiting his friends' homes in their absences. He was always suspicious of what the friend's wife would encourage him to do if he maintained a very close relationship with the wife in the absence of her husband.

He also avoided extending alms to any one of his friends' wives, all in fear of how they would interpret his alms. All of this was based on the past, as he lived in constant fear of women in general.

CHAPTER 15

TARAPUL AND KUTAR IN THE U.S.A

This was Tarapul's life before he ever left Liberia to visit the U.S. in October 1989 for the first time when war broke out in that country, forcing him to leave behind Alicia and their three kids.

At first, he thought that the war would end very soon for him to return, but month after month went by and the situation only got worse and worse. While he struggled with the idea of going back to his family, it seemed impossible or unnecessary to do so when his company, and every other major company in the country, were all closing or scaling down work, leaving most employees jobless. He thought remaining in the U.S. was the best option for now.

To remain there would require him to have a permanent U.S. status, so he met a beautiful Liberian woman named Kutar, who had just become a U.S. citizen and was capable of helping him obtain a Green Card through spouse petitioning.

He was very happy, because he believed he had got an educated type of woman that he wished to have long ago when he had to go through a compulsory marriage for impregnating Alicia.

Kutar heard the two Liberian guys talk about the war in their country while they walked past her in Walmart in New York, so she greeted them. "Hello, my brothers."

"Yeh…hello, sister." They replied.

"Are you a Liberian?" Tarapul asked her when he recognized her accent.

"Yes, I'm, that's why I said brothers to you guys." She replied.

So, they began to chat about the mess that was going on in their country, and at the end, Tarapul asked for Kutar's number to see if he could talk with her another time. She gave her number and said bye to them.

Before the day ended, he gave her a call and told her she was very pretty (you know how women feel very good when you tell them that they're very beautiful, but men understand it as the best way to start up an I-want-you conversation) and he told her that he would like to have lunch with her tomorrow. She accepted right away and the next day, they were together for lunch, which ended with a visit to her four-room apartment.

Actually, after she heard him say in Walmart that he was here on a visitor's visa and that he was confused over whether to go back or not, she thought he was vulnerable to having any woman who wanted to marry him. She also believed that he could be a perfect guy for her, because she could use him to raise more income for herself. That's why she took him home to see her place right away, so he could come by any time, whenever he wanted to.

Her expectation of a marriage proposal from him came in right away, within two weeks' time.

So, they started a relationship in a month's time with an agreement to marry him. In two months' time, he moved into her apartment, but he had no job yet.

She worked full-time at a hospital as a clinician, so she agreed to take up their financial responsibility, including the wedding preparation and the filing of a Green Card with the U.S. Immigration office for him.

Tarapul had a short-term work permit to get a job, so he got two part-time jobs in no distant time, one at a Meat Factory and another at a Paper Company. At this point, everything seemed fine, but not too long would things begin to turn sour for Tarapul.

The relationship now appeared to be for two opposite reasons: Kutar was all about finances, as she believed that Tarapul was not well-intentioned about the relationship, but he just needed a relationship to get U.S. status.

In an actual sense, Tarapul loved her, so he thought he had gotten the type of woman he had long wanted: a woman who was educated, reasonable, and would assist him in better decision-making. So, at first, there was this joy of having a classic girl, a civilized girl, an industrial girl, a girl of his type, and all descriptions of a woman of epitome. But, right now, every description has started to appear like devil water or a mirage.

For the first time meeting in her house, Kutar gave all the reasons she needed a man: she needed a man with love and commitment, a man to partner up with by sharing responsibilities in all things like house chores, rent, bills, investments, and all. Then she offered her promises, such as reciprocating her husband's love, care, and kindness, never cheating, never abusing, and sharing responsibilities.

She made it clearer that when she said sharing responsibilities, she was talking about an African man who was flexible enough to help his wife with house chores and cooking work, but not the kind of African man who makes the wife alone perform all house duties even while he was sitting at home doing nothing.

When Tarapul heard all of this, he said to her: "That's great. I like that." Then he repeated after her to say the same things to her but added, "I don't like secrets. I like openness. I like a woman who doesn't keep old boyfriends when she's married." Then she conceded and said to him like a confession, "I've gone around and have all the experiences I think I need to say that I want to have a husband to leave this thing called go-here-and- come-here." Ummmm, it's like a couple taking vows in front of the presiding pastor and the congregation, but hey, they were making these promises without even tasting the apples they have.

Now they were married and Kutar remained the highest earner, so she used her financial position for suppression. She shut him out whenever there was a financial issue and threatened to divorce him whenever he tried to make any objection to her suggestions or opinions on what, how, or when to spend it. There was no respect for him. He was like trash to her. She knew no word of apology, so he apologized for whatever the case was.

He felt tortured and intimidated, all because she thought that his life of staying in the U.S. depended on her giving him a permanent residence status.

Against all the promises, she didn't cook, she didn't do house chores, she didn't honor whatever he said, she gave him excuses as many times as it may to get away to receive or make calls each time they stayed together, she used money whenever she wanted without letting him know. I mean, she was authoritative and loved to be the boss.

Poor Tarapul. He still loved her, but he was very confused and wondered. Why he was so unlucky with getting his choice of wife?

He thought that even as well-traveled as Kutar said she was, she was still unromantic. Kissing and playing were not in her love book. He thought being with her in bed was lonesome. He said, "It's a situation where a husband and wife turn back-to-back in bed, or the worst-case scenario is when a couple refuses to cuddle because one fears that the next person would ask for what the other doesn't want to give."

He thought that this educated woman was equally behaving like the uneducated woman when it came to their sex lifestyle and sex starvation is not an exception.

He wondered what a healthy young lady thought of keeping her husband for as long as two to three weeks before service. He wanted to know what was wrong. He always felt pushed by his wife to do the things he hated to do.

He even thought that he had become the African wife in the home who did every cooking and house chores (washing, cleaning, and mopping), as well as serving her on the table, clearing plates and glasses after every meal every single day, while she sat as his husband, or worst, his boss, who gave orders like, *give-me-that* and *bring-me-that-other- one*.

No matter how tired Tarapul was in the morning, he got up early, leaving her in bed to make breakfast for them and served her breakfast in bed.

Now, he felt that in her vocabulary of a husband's love, there must be worship and total surrender to a wife.

Clearly, Tarapul thought she had violated every vow she had made to him. She had chosen the path of doing all those things she hated to be done unto her. Now, he called this behavior towards him as abuse.

Tarapul thought he was abused by a woman once again, like those who raped him or lured him. He had no peace in his mind, and he had never been in peace since the first rape by his cousin while he was 12.

Every day, he soliloquized: *Is this my portion of life? I mean to say, is this the way God destined me to be married? Is marriage worth it even while promiscuity is a sin?*

So, he cried: Tarapul, Oh - Tarapul, Oh!!!

Chapter 16

Discussion Questions

Apart from Tarapul telling me this story, I have been on the side of dialogue. This is one nature of mine that some people hate about me, because they say I argue very much, but I always tell them that argument is my way of finding answers to the things that baffle my mind, such as questions #36 and #37 in the below. It means that I love to hear what others think about a particular situation, and by that, we all can find a better way of solving a particular problem of importance. This is why, at the end of Tarapul's dilemma, I drew out a list of questions for our discussion.

Therefore, I would appreciate it very much if you could send me an email at tarslehpaul@ymail.com or to my Facebook page to share with me your answer(s) to any of the following questions as you read this book:

1. Did Everee do the right thing by turning Tarapul down after all that long time?

2. What could have been the reason Marybel left the village the next day and why she didn't repeat this act again to Tarapul?

3. Tarapul's friend, Janet, was dead, but he saw her every night in his sleep. Do you think this is true, that dead people do come back?

4. What comparison and contrast do you have for Marybel and Tybet for the rape on Tarapul?

5. Why did Tybet's dying old fiancé bend on marrying her, even when he knew his own time of departure?

6. How did Janet and Tybet become Tarapul's quest?

7. Was Tarapul truly insane to keep on chasing a girl like Everee, who always disgraced him regardless of who was observing?

8. Did Everee have legitimate reasons for her behavior towards boys?

9. Was Tarapul wrong about wanting to have his way with Everee for the first time of her visit?

10. Do you have an idea why Marybel did what she did to Tarapul?

11. What would you have done next after Everee turned you down and never wanted to see you again?

12. What do you think of Nancia?

13. In the Bible, what type of sin (conscious or unconscious) did Tarapul commit when he said to himself that Nancia was a married woman?

14. What do you think the writer means when he says: "opposite sex lurks themselves under a secret tree"?

15. Tarapul chose Mr. Silwon's wife, knowing fully well that Silwon was very jealous of his wife. What was he thinking?

16. You are a young and innocent girl, and the older man, not your uncle or relative, starts to give you gifts. What do you think about that?

17. How can you describe Lehana in Beaticer and Tarapul's situation?

18. Did Tarapul help Mr. Silwon because he was too old and weak, or he was there for other reasons?

19. What lesson did Beaticer teach all men from her affair with Tarapul?

20. What lesson can women learn from Lehana's act of taking over Beaticer's boyfriend?

21. What did the writer mean when remembering Bible Joseph's story?

22. How does this book help all men see what their actions do in their marriages?

23. As a woman, what do you make of Bonenoh's behavior when Tarapul visited his friend? Even the fish she sent the next day and the one she brought on Wednesday.

24. What would you say the relationship between Bonenoh and Yannaton was before Tarapul?

25. Tarapul said married women groomed him, so he had no fear of taking anyone down. Is he right to think that?

26. Tarapul said married women put up false smiles after all the dirty things. Was he right to have been afraid of marriage?

27. What does the writer mean by "journey of a night walk in the jungle of marriage"?

28. If you were Alicia, would you have stayed in the room with Tarapul on that day her little brother let him in?

29. Did Alicia cause this pregnancy from that night Tarapul first entered her room?

30. Alicia let Tarapul commit multiple adultery. Why?

31. Why did Bonenoh beg to be Tarapul's second wife?

32. Was he right about Bonenoh as cunning?

33. What were Tarapul's regrets about Alicia?

34. Do you think your husband feels jealous of you?

35. Why did Tarapul stay in fear of young boys?

36. Bonenoh kept Tarapul in her mind all the time as a ready-to-screw any time in sight. Does it mean that Tarapul was an ex to her?

37. From this story, who can we say is an ex?

38. Why did Tarapul refuse to go to any friend's house in his absence, even if he knew the friend's wife was alone?

39. Why do you think Kutar treated Tarapul the way she did?

40. Tarapul said Kutar was abusing him. Was he right about this?

41. Do you believe that multiple rapes turned Tarapul into a womanizer?

42. Do you think Kutar was ready for marriage?

43. Why did Kutar always hide her phone conversations?

44. What was exceptionally different between Kutar and Alicia, the two women Tarapul married at different times?

45. What kind of man do you think Tarapul was? Given that he hated what he loved to do.

46. What did you learn about the human heart and the mouth when you see the falsehoods in Kutar's promises to Tarapul?

47. How can we explain the Bible point that talks about what comes from the mouth defiles a person when we think of Kutar's promises and failures? (Read Matt. 15:18 ESV)

48. Do you sense that Tarapul has been stigmatized over the years?

49. Before Tarapul told me, the writer and author of this book, he had so much gone on in his mind. He thought his story was worth telling for several reasons. What do you think his main reason was?

CHAPTER 17

TYPES OF RAPE AND IMPACTS

I was already working on my Spiritual book before Tarapul told me his story, so I took much interest in it because of two reasons:

- As a male human being, I have had similar experiences with women, particularly around marriage.

I was also raped by a married woman who used me as a tool. She also inherited me from her friend the same night her friend left the house to go visit a relative out of town, but never returned due to family matters.

- The most important reason I took this story is because of the spiritual revelation attached to it that I want to explain, which has to do with heavenly judgment matter. That is: a lot of us human beings coerce (force) other people against

their will in this world. One of such is women
forcing men to have something to do with them.

Isn't it true that all over the world, radio & television news emphasize how men rape women, but say little about what women do? As women's issues become highly important to the people of this world, the opposite is God's stance.

The reason is simple. God has seen how much damage women have done to the churches since they (Spiritual women) left Heaven and came to fight men (Spiritual men) on Earth, who were maltreating physical women through the instruments of physical men on earth.

This matter of women raping men has become so important to God to discuss, because a lot of his servants (pastors whose hearts He sees from above) have been conquered in this way by beautiful women. This means that these women often choose to bring down some men who choose righteousness, so much so that they think those pastors are perfecting themselves above other men.

He tells me (even as I am writing tonight in November 2019, His spirit is still speaking to me) that there are a few men of God who truly love God and have resolved to do the right thing, but as soon as any of them touches a woman, he becomes useless in his spirit (soul) and has become like all others who desire the flesh so much that they begin to serve the little gods. Serving these little gods starts with worshipping money and loving women so much.

It is due to this fact that God gave me the third category of sin that appeared in the Bible, but was never discussed. It is that "Imposed sin" that we shall explain in all its forms Starting with what the women in this book have done to the young man called "Tarapul," who complained to God several times and asked questions about this kind of behavior.

And even while we discuss this sin type, we may also look at another topic, like Lehana's statement of God in this book. At one point, she said, "God had made it possible for Beaticer to leave so that Lehana would get Tarapul for herself."

Now, the question is: Is there God's involvement here? Was it God that was putting all those thoughts in her head as to how to lure Tarapul into bed even while her friend, Beaticer, was still there? Let's find time to discuss more of this and the third sin category.

Now, that we're discussing rape, which is physical in nature, it's time for God wants to reveal Spiritual rape as well. But, before we talk about it, let's study how sex is handled in Heavens, the Spirit world:

Right And Wrong About Sex

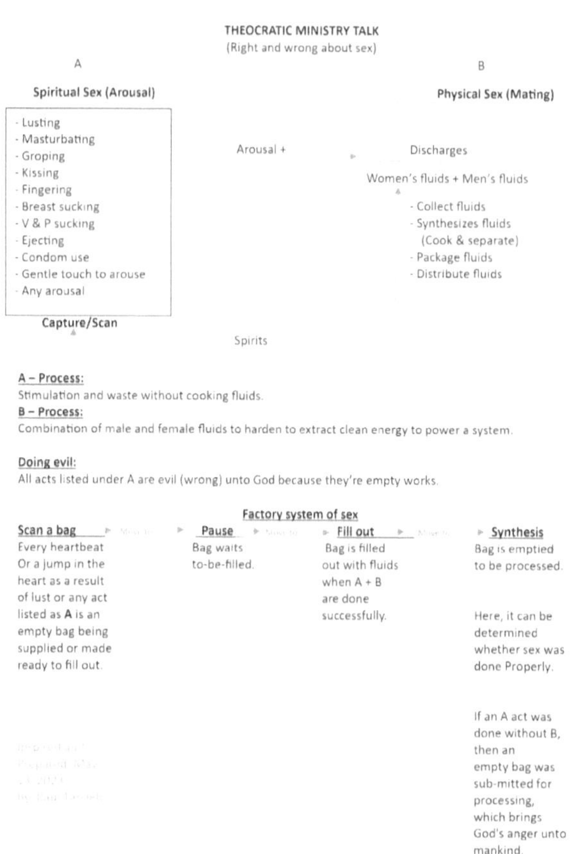

This table explains how the spirits handle sex.

From the table above, we can see words like lusting, groping, kissing, and others listed left for arousal, while mating (genital contacts) involving the discharge of fluids is listed right for physical sex.

Arousal is the main word God wants to reveal to us. It is an action affecting Spiritual forces (spirits) that oversee sex, which are acting forces called sexual spirits. They operate many departments.

Arousal – can simply be defined as awakening power. It means that the spirits (forces) of sex can be awakened by our actions performed on earth. Our actions are ignited by what goes on in the heart.

The relationship everyone's actions have with his/her heart can best be explained from a diagram called the *Information Superhighway*. The Information Superhighway explains how information leaves every human's heart to go to the Heavens and vice versa, and what happens to that information en route to Heaven.

Based on the relationship between the human heart and the Spirit world, God was able to reveal in the Bible that lust is sex, which means that whenever a person lusts in his/her heart, he/she has had sex with the other person already.

The Bible says **lust** is an act of a person (originally referring to male) looking at any woman and having the feeling of having sexual intercourse with that woman. In a 2008 reveal of the same word, lust, the Spirit of God revealed that in some extreme cases, some men gain an erection right away just by looking at any woman who appeals to their desire.

The reason God (the Bible) said that is found under the A column of the table above. Looking at the bottom of the "A" listed words, you'll find the word "Scan/Capture."

This explains that as soon as a man lusts (his eyes blink and his heart jumps) after seeing a woman who appeals to his eyes very much, the heart of that man captures his appeal right away and sends it to the Spirit realm as a request or a trigger or a provocation or an invocation for the sex spirits to come to work.

Modern science & technology can now explain to us quickly how fast these actions connect to one another – from eye sighting to heart beating to spirit descension and ascension. Imagine how fast your voice on a phone is traveling between terminals carrying your voice to bring the next person's voice.

So, as soon as a man lusts after a woman (the same as with a woman these days), the sex spirit automatically descends to earth to capture/scan from the heart of the man and takes it up into the Spirit world in the form of a load or a bag that was prepared in the heart of a person. That's why every lust, grope, kiss, masturbation, breast sucking, and all listed under A are considered Spiritual sex since they bring down spirit beings to collect loads, regardless of what is in each bag of load.

So, what's the difference between Spiritual sex and physical sex?

Well, the Spiritual sex simply prepares bags or containers that need to be filled out, while the physical sex brings in the fluids from a male and a female to fill the bags/ containers.

So, let's go back to the table once again to see column B. Under column B, you can see the word "Discharges", which means when a male and a female mate together (connect their genitals), it is expected of them to produce a mixture of two fluids that are taken to Heaven as a single dose of a liquid, which must be emptied into the containers that were prepared earlier during all the kissing, and every fondling acts carried on prior to genital connection.

Therefore, it can be said that sex comprises two parts: one

part (arousal) prepares storage materials in the Spirit realm that human beings have nothing to do with, while the other part (genital connection) produces two fluids needed by the Spirit to have energy for themselves.

The entire concept can be understood by studying why God created human beings to eat the plants and animals of the earth, and He required them to keep their body holy or clean. Apart from the sexual fluids from males and females, the purpose of blood can also be derived from the same study, which is why Satan needs more blood all the time, which lies behind the many wars that Satan provokes in the human world.

Therefore, the major purpose of this book is not only to encourage men to report their own rape cases but to reveal Spiritual rape as well since God will judge perpetrators and rape victims differently based on what He knows.